Veritas Book Shop
7-8 Lower Abbey St
Dublin 1
Tel: 018788177
www.veritas.ie
VAT No. IE8T47036A

Tip: 00000P0005000040880
Staff: Dione   Trans: 41899
Date: 26/04/19 15:27

Description   Amount

Item No.: 9781847306368
Learning to Love pcs   9.99 A

Total Eur   9.99
Cash   -10.00

Rounding   0.01

VAT%	Net.Amt	VAT	Amount
0	9.99	0.00	9.99

Returns accepted with 28 days only
in saleable condition and with receipt
This does not affect your statutory
rights
Thank you for shopping with Veritas

T 0 1 0 5 0 0 0 0 4 1 8 9 9

of God's children on the last day, and the view is stunning: 'On the rock too high for me to reach, set me on high' (Psalms 60:3). As stated previously, Our Lady's glorious state doesn't make her distant from us; on the contrary, she is closer to us than any earthly mother could ever be, and she desires us to find the way to heaven, who is her Son. Jesus prayed to the Father, just before his death: 'Father, I want those you have given me to be with me where I am, so that they may always see the glory you have given me' (John 17:24). He certainly wanted Mary – his own mother and first disciple – to be with him; he ardently wants each of us to be with him, one day, in joyful, endless celebration of love.

5. Mary is Crowned as Queen: Happy Endings (Isaiah 60:1-7)

'Arise, shine out, for your light has come': Mary has come home. Her radiant beauty, already manifested on earth, even in a hidden life, now appears in the fullness of divine splendour. If the saints reflect 'like mirrors the brightness of the Lord' (2 Corinthians 3:18), how much more the Queen of all saints must shine out with God's glory. Glory means the revealing of God's love; Mary's life on earth was all love, entirely at the loving service of his children – and she continues to serve God's children as our shining star, so that we might never give up before reaching our goal. Like any mother, her main concern in life was her son; because she knew in faith that every person was in his image, she truly saw his face in everyone she met. She reigns now as Queen because she served and loved; when we pray to her, she enables us to serve with love, and to see the face of Jesus in those we meet.

If a painter showed you their masterpiece, you'd certainly admire it. If a poet read you their best poem, you'd be all ears. You know instinctively that your admiration for the work bestows praise on the artist. When we contemplate Mary, we see God's *chef-d'œuvre*, the greatest work of his grace; the honour we show her glorifies the Creator. We need never fear that devotion to Mary could somehow detract from giving praise to God. This way of looking applies to all the saints, and by analogy, can help us to see others in a new light. Saint Paul reminds us that 'we are God's work of art' (Ephesians 2:10); the Greek word used is the origin of the word 'poem'. Looking upon each person as a fresh artistic creation of the Lord changes the way we see the world.

What is love anyway?

One of Jesus' most important sayings is found in St John's Gospel: 'If you make my word your home, you will indeed be my disciples, you will learn the truth, and the truth will make you free' (8:31-32). Praying the Rosary gradually allows his Word to take root in us. We learn the truth about our lives, that we are loved and called to glory, and this sets us free from our own negativity and from the false gods offered by society. Saint Augustine says, 'There is not one who does not love something, but the question is, what to love. We cannot love unless someone has loved us first' (cf. 1 John 4:10).

If we don't always have warm feelings of love and tenderness towards others, we can take heart from the words of St Thomas Aquinas: 'to love means to consistently will and choose the good of the other'. Knowing we are loved unconditionally, walking on a path from darkness to light, we *can* learn to love because he loved us first. 'He brought me forth into freedom, he saved me because he loved me' (Psalms 17:20).

Departure Lounge

A priest working as a hospital chaplain once said to me, 'All my clients in the departure lounge have their boarding passes!' I have great admiration for hospital chaplains and healthcare workers; the stamina required for being present at life's critical moments can never be taken for granted. All of us have known many acquaintances that have passed through the 'departure lounge'. In fact, our existence often seems made up of a dreary series of farewells. I was twelve years old the first time I saw someone die before my eyes. After watching a soccer match (Ipswich Town beating Arsenal in the Cup Final), I walked up to the High Street to wait for a bus, to visit my favourite record shop. Opposite the bus stop was a row of neat little houses, which are still there today. A man opened his front door, walked into his garden and promptly collapsed on the path. An ambulance arrived; he was pronounced dead at the scene. I was certainly shaken up; the kindly ambulance driver took me home. Only years later, when I put together a notebook with anniversary dates in it, did I find the exact date (since it was Cup Final day), and wrote, 'Man at bus stop, 1978.' He may not have had anyone praying for him at his last moments, but the Lord can backdate our prayers. The good news is that in heaven, there are no more departures: only arrivals, until the full number of saints is complete, and then the party will really begin.

Pilgrims to Lourdes sometimes hear cited Our Lady's words to St Bernadette: 'I cannot promise you happiness in this life; only in the next'. A priest in Lourdes once explained that this doesn't necessarily imply an unhappy life on earth, rather that the more we tend toward the *next* life, the more we will find happiness here and now. Saint Bernadette herself wrote: 'How happy my soul was, good Mother, when I had the good fortune to gaze upon you! You, the Queen of heaven and earth, deigned to make use of the most fragile thing in the world's eyes'. This brings us back to our original question, finding our heart's desire. The psalmist suggests an answer: 'There is one thing I ask of the Lord, for this I long, to live in the house of the Lord, all the days of my life' (Psalms 26:4). Having begun our journey sitting at home, we are led through the various stages of life to *the house of the Lord*, where Mary reigns as Queen. The Rosary gains us access to this happy place; meditating the Gospel with Our Lady gives us a foretaste of the next life, where our heart's desire will be granted and all our expectations will be infinitely exceeded.

World on Fire

Saint Catherine of Siena famously said, 'Be who God meant you to be and you will set the world on fire.' This is nothing less than holiness, becoming saints. But it's not an instant process. I sometimes admit in talks to young people that my goal in life is to become a holy old priest. Once, a girl answered rather cheekily, 'You are already, Father!' I'm not sure exactly what she meant, but reaching the halfway stage of my active priestly ministry this year (assuming I retire at seventy-five), I have to say it's not happening as quickly as I'd like, this holiness business (growing older seems to be taking care of itself). The good news is that walking on this journey with Mary helps to keep us young, for she is 'younger than sin,' as Georges Bernanos wrote, referring to her Immaculate Conception. The more people there are who pray the Rosary, allowing Mary's heart to inflame them with God's love, the more the world will be set on fire with his love. We oldies might feel slightly jealous of the young saints – those who left an indelible mark of the Lord's presence on this earth in a very brief space of time – but God knows what he's doing. St Thérèse of Lisieux, St Elizabeth of the Trinity, Blessed Pier-Giorgio Frassati, St Kateri Tekakwitha and many others were taken up before the age of thirty; the world would have been much poorer without them. A personal favourite, Blessed Chiara Badano (1971–90), is as far as I know the first person born after me already beatified, by Pope Benedict in 2010. This smiling Italian teenager, who serenely accepted bone cancer with loving faith, has already inspired so many young believers. Along with the many contemporary saints and witnesses whose lives we gradually discover, may her prayers bring many of our young people to discover Christ, his amazing plans for them, and his gift to them (and to all of us) of Mary, Mother of Mercy and Queen of Apostles. 'They shall tell of the Lord to generations yet to come, declare his faithfulness to peoples yet unborn: "These things the Lord has done"' (Psalms 21:31-32). May the next generation of saints bring even greater glory to God and set the world on fire.

Conclusion: On the lips of children

The last word should go to one of the little saints whose presence brightened up many lives. Bernie was a very wise and joyful lady with Down Syndrome, now gone to the Lord. One day she was there for a Mass I was celebrating in a small chapel. My homily was just starting to take off (I used to preach for a longer period of time in those days, before it occurred to me that priests probably spend their purgatory listening to their own homilies, end-to-end). As I paused for breath at the end of a particularly punchy sentence, a small but firm voice came from the back of the chapel: 'AMEN!' It was Bernie. Cue general laughter; there wasn't much point in continuing. Surely the Lord was saying to me: that's enough. 'On the lips of children and of babes you have found praise' (Psalms 8:3). Thank you, Lord, for the people you send us to show your love for us, and to remind us not to take ourselves too seriously. Thank you for telling us, 'See that you never despise any of these little ones, for I tell you that their angels in heaven are continually in the presence of my Father in heaven' (Matthew 18:10). May our prayer and our attention to others foster our lifelong quest for learning to love and help us grow in authentic, 'evangelical' peace, so that we become real peacemakers for our world.

As St John Paul II wrote in *Rosarium Virginis Mariae*, 40:

> *The Rosary is by its nature a prayer for peace*, since it consists in the contemplation of Christ, the Prince of Peace, the one who is 'our peace' (Ephesians 2:14). Anyone who assimilates the mystery of Christ – and this is clearly the goal of the Rosary – learns the secret of peace and makes it his life's project. Moreover, by virtue of its meditative character, with the tranquil succession of *Hail Marys*, the Rosary has a peaceful effect on those who pray it, disposing them to receive and experience in their innermost depths, and to spread around them, that true peace which is the special gift of the Risen Lord (cf. John 14:27; 20:21).

POSTSCRIPT

Open Your Lips and Let God's Word Be Heard

We must always meditate on God's wisdom, keeping it in our hearts and on our lips. Your tongue must speak justice; the law of God must be in your heart. Hence, Scripture tells you: You shall speak of these commandments when you sit in your house, and when you walk along the way, and when you lie down, and when you get up. Let us then speak of the Lord Jesus, for he is wisdom, he is the word, the Word indeed of God.

It is also written: Open your lips, and let God's word be heard. God's word is uttered by those who repeat Christ's teaching and meditate on his sayings. Let us always speak this word. When we speak about wisdom, we are speaking of Christ. When we speak about virtue, we are speaking of Christ. When we speak about justice, we are speaking of Christ. When we speak about peace, we are speaking of Christ. When we speak about truth and life and redemption, we are speaking of Christ.

Open your lips, says Scripture, and let God's word be heard. It is for you to open; it is for him to be heard. So, David said: I shall hear what the Lord says in me. The very Son of God says: Open your lips, and I will fill them. Not all can attain to the perfection of wisdom as Solomon or Daniel did, but the spirit of wisdom is poured out on all according to their capacity, that is, on all the faithful. If you believe, you have the spirit of wisdom.

Meditate, then, at all times on the things of God, and speak the things of God, when you sit in your house. By house we can understand the Church, or the secret place within us, so that we are to speak within ourselves. Speak with prudence, so as to avoid falling into sin, as by excess of talking. When you sit in your house, speak to yourself as if you were a judge. When you walk along the way, speak, so as never to be idle. You speak along the way if you speak in Christ, for Christ is the way. When you walk along the way, speak to yourself, speak to Christ. Hear him say to you: 'I desire that in every place men should pray, lifting holy hands without anger or quarrelling'. When you lie down, speak so that the sleep of death may not steal upon you. Listen and learn how you are to speak as you lie down; I will not give sleep to my eyes or slumber to my eyelids until I find a place for the Lord, a dwelling place for the God of Jacob.

When you get up or rise again, speak of Christ, so as to fulfil what you are commanded. Listen and learn how Christ is to awaken you from sleep. Your soul says: I hear my brother knocking at the door. Then Christ says to you: Open the door to me, my sister, my spouse. Listen and learn how you are to awaken Christ. Your soul says: I charge you, daughters of Jerusalem, awaken or reawaken the love of my heart. Christ is that love.

Saint Ambrose, Explanations of the Psalms
(From the Office of Readings, Liturgy of the Hours-
Thursday, week 6 of Ordinary Time)

To contact the author, email: nigel.woollen@gmail.com

THE LAMB WILL CONQUER

Reflections on the Knock Apparition

Nigel Woollen

'I never knew what depth and richness there was to the Knock apparition until I read Fr Woollen's wonderful book. His reflections are richly biblical, insightful, down to earth, and applicable to daily Christian life. He shows that Knock has a very important message for pilgrims and all believers today – one that can move us to a deeper love for Christ and awareness of his power at work in us.'

Dr Mary Healy, PhD
Professor, Sacred Heart Major Seminary, Detroit
Member of the Pontifical Biblical Commission

'Fr Nigel Woollen guides us gently into the "divine secret" of silence at the heart of the Knock Apparition. His book of reflections has something wonderful to offer to everyone, whether they are visiting for the first time or regard Knock a second home.'

Ms Breda O'Brien
Journalist and teacher, Dublin

'Read it through; then start over and reflect on it all again: *The Lamb Will Conquer* invites us inwards, to contemplate the deep mysteries at the heart of the Knock apparition.'

Most Rev. Eamon Martin
Archbishop of Armagh & Primate of All Ireland